# Everything I Know

By Paul Jarvis

D1604114

Paul Jarvis, Author

Cheri Hanson, Editor

Marc Johns, Cover Illustration

978-0991918614, ISBN

Portions of this book have appeared on my mailing list (pjrvs.com/signup) over the last few years.

**Other books by Paul Jarvis**

*Eat Awesome*

www.eatawesome.ca

*Be Awesome at Online Business*

www.pjrvs.com/book

*Write & Sell Your Damn Book*

www.mydamnbook.com

# Contents

# Foreword

*By Justine Musk*

I have a confession to make. As delighted as I am to write this foreword, I'm handing it in later than I said I would. I could rustle up some excuse (a serious case of strep-throat-complicated-by-crap-I-breathed-in-at-Burning-Man) or plead the Flaky Artist Defense, which god knows I've done before, but truth is it's just downright unprofessional of me. It feels more so because I'm handing it in to Paul Jarvis, who is the ultimate pro. The dude is so fast that he's responding to your email before you've even sent it.

By the time I stumbled across Paul, he had figured out his story, which is a slightly more poetic way of saying that he knew who he was (online) and what he was doing (online). This was good for me, because I myself did not. I had been 'blogging' on LiveJournal for several years. I moved to wordpress.com thinking it was wordpress.org or not understanding the difference between them. After mutilating a template or four, I knew enough to develop a proper case of what Marie Forleo calls "website shame." I needed a doctor, stat.

Paul's story is, like all the best stories, baked into his product. He markets himself through his work. It tells his story for him. After months of investigating the designs of various websites, I came back to the first blog that had visually resonated with me. It belonged to one Danielle LaPorte. A closer examination revealed the name of its maker. In the spirit of a writer who would like to be a rock star, but lacked actual musical talent, I went to Paul with the idea that I wanted my blog to feel like an album cover. When I found out that Paul was in a band, I figured that he was my guy. (Eventually my blog would have a black-and-white header of me posing topless, albeit tastefully, with a yellow ball python. His name was Angelo.)

Once we'd unveiled my new website, an interesting thing happened. Having a stronger visual sense of who I was (online) and what I stood for – my 'brand' – worked its way into my writing. I grew bolder. I began to steer my subject matter away from what I'd been talking about... to what I really wanted to talk about. My traffic increased. I became better known.

Although website design is something Paul does, it is not his real business. He's in the creativity and self-discovery business. He's in the finding-your-voice business. He understands that we want to do great work, that there's a story struggling to speak through us, not just about who we are, but about who our clients or customers or readers want to be and how we can best help them become that. He doesn't try to tell it for us. He asks questions and provides advice, tools and insights to unlock our story and let it flow.

That's why this book doesn't claim to be a blueprint for success. Just like you can't express your unique value when you're copying someone else's website, you can't develop a stand-out brand and play to your own strengths and values if you're copying someone else's marketing, tactics and strategy. We all have our heroes, our role models, the people we look up to, but as Paul himself points out, we have to treat them as starting points that launch us more deeply into ourselves. Instead of trying to be more like them, we have to take note of those places where we can't be – and then jump into those places, and build out from there. We leave the borrowed blueprints behind, and rely instead on our inner strengths, our deeper wisdom. That's how we come to be original.

*Easier said than done.*

I'm often struck by the way people will toss off the advice to *just be yourself* without acknowledging that this is a slippery and complicated mission. It requires a vulnerability that our culture has trained us to avoid, so much so that we construct an entire 'false self' to protect our tender souls. In order to just be yourself, you have to crack apart that persona and expose the meat of who you are. You need the skills, and enough mastery of your craft, to project that truth of self in your work. When the gap between who you are and the projection of who you are (your 'personal brand') is as narrow as possible, you ring true. We call you authentic, and are that much more likely to engage with you or do business with you.

Which is why the best stories don't play off, and market to, our sense of inadequacy, but inspire us into a bigger, truer version of ourselves – a greater sense of the possible. You empower your clients by casting them as the hero of the story instead of you or the product or service that you wish to sell them (that would supposedly sweep in and solve all their problems). You cast yourself as the mentor. Your role is to provide the hero with advice, tools, gifts and insights to aid them in their quest for self-actualization.

That's what Paul does. That's who he is. Like any good mentor, he's been there and done that, and he's brought back a few things to teach us.

So I wish you all the best with your own story, and I'm glad that this book, this foreword, is a part of it.

May you truly be yourself. May you be yourself on purpose. May your story be epic, your voice be true, and your business be badass. Paul Jarvis would tell you to settle for nothing less.

It's good advice. I think you should take it.

# Introduction

I'm afraid of being arrested by the Creative Police.

They'll receive an urgent tip that I'm to be immediately brought up on fraud charges. They'll break through the front door of my house and drag me kicking and screaming (more like sobbing uncontrollably) from my bed.

I'll be tried in a court of my peers, or at least by a jury of Twitter followers. They'll show, in painstaking detail, that I don't know anything; that I should never give another human being advice, and that everything I've created is utter garbage. There'll be pie charts and expert witnesses. My expensive lawyer will spend most of the trial with her face buried in her hands, unable to raise any objections. The evidence against me will be so clear that the judge will start playing Angry Birds.

I'll be sentenced to wear a suit and tie in some beige office with a non-ironic water cooler. I'll get four or five consecutive life terms, with no chance of parole. No visitation rights, either. I'll never see my wife and pet rats again.

I've played this scenario out in my head many times.

In reality, I wake every morning without a warrant for my arrest. I'm free to go about my day and create new things. I'm free to share those things with the world, and to risk it all and do my work. So that's what I do.

My goal for this book is to illustrate the potential you've got inside you, right now, to do something unique and innovative. I know this because I have that same potential, and I struggle to let it out sometimes. You won't know how far your potential reaches until you start experimenting with it and pushing its boundaries.

I create things I'm scared as hell to share all the time, but I keep sharing them. I continue to make my own path in whatever I do, because I know it's the only way to be truly happy with what I create. I try new things and constantly push myself because even though the Creative Police are always watching (possibly from that unmarked van across the street), I'm addicted to seeing how far I can take my work and how often I can experiment with new ideas. That's how I find the most meaning in what I make. I don't enjoy that nervous feeling in my gut, but I'm genuinely curious about how far I can go.

This book is my challenge to you to take your own risks and stretch your own limits. Courage doesn't come from an absence of fear; it comes from being afraid and moving forward anyway. I want you to see how far you can go. I challenge to you to stir shit up.

I've created my business in my own unique way (without a criminal record) for almost two decades. And if this doesn't work out, who knows, maybe we'll even share a prison cell. But at least we'll have taken a risk and tried to create something great and meaningful.

## It's adventure time

Long before I started working for myself and having visions of police raids, I loved reading *Choose Your Own Adventure* novels.

If you aren't familiar with this series (published by Bantam Books in the 1980s & 1990s), they put you, the reader, into the story and let you determine the plot. You're the hero, in charge of making decisions and you're constantly confronted with choices.

Say you're off to save the princess (the books were unfortunately gender biased) and you came upon a dragon guarding the path. If you wanted to fight, you'd turn to page 13. If you wanted to pivot and run, you'd turn to page 18.

Each choice would lead you to a different page and eventually, to a unique ending where you'd either succeed (and save that princess) or fail (and get eaten by the dragon).

I loved these books because I got to lead the action and I could always see the consequences of my choices. The plot wasn't set in stone until I was actually in the story, reading it, deciding. The ending was never certain, but in order to get there, I had to keep making choices.

Two people could read the same book and come away with totally different experiences, adventures and endings. You could also get stuck in plot loops that kept you in an unbreakable cycle until you made a different choice.

I've always approached my work as if it were a *Choose Your Own Adventure* book. And if I look at how I live, the parallels are evident:

*I choose my own path.*

*I stay true to myself and to my values.*

*I experiment with choices.*

*I might be afraid, but I don't let fear stop me from trying new things.*

*I can only live a meaningful life if I keep making choices and moving forward, pushing past my fears and testing my limits.*

We all face challenges (or dragons) on our paths —whether they're paths we're forging or well-worn routes others have taken. It's okay if you're scared to do new things or to put your work out in the world, because I am too. But, I keep making choices, moving forward and creating my own adventure, day by day. I hope this book will inspire you to do the same.

## My one & only real job

I haven't always been self-employed. I was a web designer for a Toronto ad agency at the beginning of my career, just to see how "work" worked. I didn't like my boss or the job, but I was grateful to learn how I *didn't* want to run my own business.

I worked hard while I was there – so much so that the day after I quit, instead of figuring out how to write a resume, I ended up answering back-to-back calls from the agency's clients. They kept asking where I was going to work next, so they could follow me there.

After the third or fourth client call, I realized that I didn't have to bring them to a new agency; I could just work for them on my own, and work in a way that made sense to me. From that point on, I knew that if I was going to be my own boss, I wanted to be a good one.

In order to be that good boss to myself, I had to be clear about what I wanted to do and how I wanted to get there. I've now spent almost two decades working for myself and building a job that I enjoy.

I've never put much stock in rules or formulas. I'd rather try things first-hand and learn from my own experiences. Sometimes I fail and I lose money or clients, but sometimes I don't. Either way, I always learn something valuable.

## More of the same, please?

Some of us have come from jobs where playing by the rules could help us get ahead. We could slowly progress to have different, bigger bosses. But, we'd still be governed by how someone else wanted to run their company, and that company might also be subject to rules enforced by investors, shareholders and boards – not to mention someone else's vision of success.

It's so easy to apply that same mentality to your own work. Maybe you believe that if you build similar products to everyone else in your industry, you can have a piece of the same pie. But, that pie has a finite number of slices, and it might not suit your tastes. Sometimes it's better just to bake a new pie. You can flavour it exactly how you want and even use a killer new recipe.

The amazing thing about working for yourself is that you don't have to follow the leader. You can carve your own path and establish your own rules. You can express your unique voice. You can align a job with your values and create work that feels fulfilling and exciting. This is, after all, the reason most people go into business for themselves in the first place.

## The dragon in the room

*This might not work.*

I can only illustrate what I've learned and what I've seen others do to achieve their goals. It's not enough to use these lessons to guide your work, though.

There are lessons in this book, for sure, but I can't stress enough that you need to experiment for yourself and forge your own path. Doing the exact opposite of everything I share could actually be what creates the most meaning in your life and work.

We don't know the consequences of our choices until those consequences become the present or the past. No one can tell you with any certainty that following specific steps will lead you to success. If someone claims to have a one-size-fits-all solution, run screaming in the other direction.

This book isn't meant to be straight-up advice. The world is full of "proven tips and tricks." Everyone's a teacher, guru, expert, or has an online course for you to follow. These experts probably (mostly) have good intentions, but they're wrong – not because the information they provide isn't sound, but because they're telling *their* stories, and sharing what worked for them and why. I'm doing the same right now.

But none of us advice-givers know what's possible for you. We can offer insight, sure, but that's about it. My best advice? *Fuck advice and listen to yourself.* Trust in your journey and learn as much as possible through first-hand experiments.

There's more than one way to reach your goals, and you probably won't even know you're on the right path until you're looking back at it.

# BOOK ONE

# Choose your own path

*"I must create a system or be enslaved by another man's;*
*I will not reason and compare: my business is to create."*

William Blake

## Your work

If I had a nickel for every time I heard, "I'd love a website just like *so-and-so's*," I'd have almost enough cash to buy a yacht.

I also see countless websites that follow the same layout as the leaders in the field, and use the same tone, the same calls to action and offer similar products. These aren't direct copies or blatant rip-offs, but they're similar enough that their owners aren't doing themselves any favours. There's nothing unique about them, so they're utterly forgettable.

While there's an obvious benefit to learning from established leaders and those who have come before you, there's no way to differentiate your work in the market if it's exactly like someone else's.

We try to emulate other people's success because it seems like the easiest and shortest path to winning at business. If they did well with a specific approach, then can't we do the same? If a map to the pot of gold is already drawn, shouldn't we just follow it? There's just one problem; the first person who arrived already grabbed that treasure. You need to go off-trail and off-map to find your own lucky charms.

The world rewards people who try things and come up with new ways of doing business. The biggest innovators get the biggest rewards, and those who simply copy the original model get only part of the original reward – at best.

I can't say this enough — you don't have to model your work on someone else's pattern, or to emulate how things typically run. And you definitely don't have to follow how big businesses operate. If you take one thing from this book, I hope it's that the adventure you choose is your own.

If there was a single business model that anyone and everyone could use to become super successful, then private jets and yachts and fancy champagne would be on back order. You'd see money fights on every corner.

So, if emulating another person guarantees nothing, then why not do things *your* way – where your way is aligned with your values and what's important to you. And if what you try doesn't work, you can always pivot or change things up. You'll be in the same market as the leaders, except you're now different from them. Win-win, right?

This is how you choose your own adventure.

## Worth & values

School teaches us to measure our worth by the grades we receive. They're assigned to us by well-meaning external sources (teachers) and we're worth more as students if we're at the top of our class.

Further along in our lives, bosses and even clients try to determine our worth by how much we sell or improve the bottom line. Our worth is also measured by how much we get paid, which is once again dictated by an external source.

I've never put much stock in this outdated system. I'd rather determine my worth internally, and the only way I know how to do that is by living my life based on what I value the most. These internal values are different for everyone, and they can certainly change as our lives evolve and grow.

If we measure our worth internally, external forces can't affect it. It can be entirely separate from how much we make or how much our work earns in the free market. For me, income falls pretty far down on the list of what I value, so money doesn't determine my worth. If it did, I'd work more so I could earn more money and therefore, feel more worthy.

If I focus on doing work that aligns with what I value, I feel like my work has meaning. If I write a book that just two people buy, but it helps them immensely, I feel like that work was worthwhile.

A large part of choosing your path is figuring out which values will determine your worth. Once that's clear, it's much easier to decide if the work you're doing will increase or decrease your feelings of worth.

# Promotion vs. doing

Having a blog isn't a business. Being you isn't a business, either. Both of those things are great, and both are important for building your brand and finding your voice. But, your brand and voice don't directly bring in money, even though they're necessary and wonderful things. You and your blog are not a business model, nor are they a substitute for doing actual, tangible, valuable work.

People often come to me thinking that a new website design will fix their sales problem. Usually, I turn down these projects because I'm not interested in putting makeup on pigs, so to speak. Dressing up a product or service won't accomplish anything unless it's already valuable. If you're focused on better promotion instead of better work, nothing will change.

Work means offering a valuable product or service – and that work has to inspire people to pay you for it. The rise of passion-driven solo entrepreneurs is great, but passion alone won't translate into money unless other people are passionate enough to open their wallets.

What you do should line up with your passion and values, sure. But it also has to be useful to others if you want to make money, and for that to happen, you have to be (or get) really damn good at it.

If people aren't paying for your work, it's not a problem you can solve with more social media promotion — it's a matter of getting better at that work by doing more of it, or finding other work that does have value to others. Social media can only amplify what's already there.

You can't "charge what you're worth" because your worth should come from an internal source. If you have lots of money, you aren't magically worth more as a human being, just like you're not worth less than anyone else if you're broke. Worth and money shouldn't be tied to each other, ever.

Sharing your passions on your blog or social media is great and it's a smart practice. I do the same by sharing what I write. But blogging and social media don't make you better at your craft; *doing your craft* makes you better at it. You can certainly use your platform to test ideas. I do it all the time. If a tweet is popular, I turn it into a blog post. If that blog post is popular, I turn it into a book chapter. That's how I write – by testing the value of my ideas before selling them as products.

Promotion is no substitute for perfecting your craft. And most people don't get paid for promoting; they get paid for doing actual work.

## Focus on the work

Choosing *my* own adventure means creating designs that help others, plus pushing my creative limits as often as possible. There are thousands of web designers and web agencies that do exactly what I do.

I don't care if I stand out or not, and I've never once promoted my web services anywhere, had business cards or made cold calls, because I'm too busy working.

I also make sure that I do what I've agreed to do – on time and on budget. No exceptions. That's what it means to do great work. It's not enough to get new clients or opportunities; you have to follow through and execute them. Every single time.

All I need to run my business is to keep helping people by doing exceptional work for them. Twitter and Facebook could break tomorrow and I wouldn't worry.

That said, I spend a lot of time writing, which is a form of promotion. I do this not to advertise my books or web services, but because I want to help others, and writing is the best way I know how to do it en masse.

So my writing is definitely promotion, but that's a side effect, not a reason I do it. I don't think I could write good sales copy to save my life. But, I do want to share what I know, and writing information- and opinion-type articles and books is the best way for me to accomplish that goal.

Writing also allows me to explore my ideas in public. I don't usually know if an idea is sound until I write about it. When I share it with someone else, they either agree or look at me sideways. If it's the latter, I re-evaluate the idea, re-evaluate whether that person is my intended audience, and sometimes I just move on.

# The business of "different"

My own business has always been unlike other web designers and agencies because I focus on clients instead of the web design industry. This is a radical difference, because my industry is so deeply introspective.

I couldn't care less about debating the latest tech trends or using the current jargon. Flat vs. skeuomorphism? Flash vs. HTML (dating myself with this)? They're all just conversations that rarely consider the end audience. I don't even care if other designers know who I am.

Instead, I focus on the people who hire web designers. I write what they want to know, I talk about my services in language they use, and I cultivate relationships by helping them succeed.

When I started doing web design, you needed to be a designer to understand most web design sites—they were full of jargon and nerdy references. Not one seemed to care about the audience and customers they served. I thought this was a horrible idea and ran in the other direction.

I try to ensure that everything I write or create makes sense to the audience I serve—which is primarily creative entrepreneurs. To truly be "experts," we have to think and speak in ways that our audience understands, because most of the time, that audience is not an expert in the same field.

Sure, it's good to keep up a little, but when industry-specific dialogue takes over, we're no longer serving our audiences. The most successful people I've worked with speak to interested consumers instead of industry peers.

## Keep questioning. Stay curious

If I had listened to "expert" advice, I might be running a large web design agency with employees, health-care packages, investors, HR consultants and probably some stupid fucking pool or foosball table for "morale." The office dog would have a bio on the website. That's not a bad thing (except for the pool table), but it's not what I want. I like to take time off—sometimes a few months a year. I like to skip work if I can and go for a hike instead. If it's sunny outside, sometimes I'd rather play in the forest than sit at a computer. I get my work done, sure, but I get it done on my own time. I would also rather do the work than manage others. Some people are remarkable managers, but I'm not one of those people.

Instead of following that expert advice, I stayed curious. I questioned everything anyone told me. I always felt I'd rather make something new that reflects who I really am than listen to "proven advice" and model what I do after someone else's success.

You stay curious by taking a beginner's mindset as often as possible. How would you approach something if you had never seen or thought about it before? A beginner's mind acknowledges that you don't know everything and still have more to learn. This attitude allows you to question even longstanding ideas and to ensure your work is aligned with your values. It also allows you to be more innovative than someone who's cynical or bored. That desire to figure everything out elevates your creativity. It's good stuff.

Only you know what fits your values and works best for your life. What has succeeded for someone else might lead you to utter failure. So why not do things your way by following your own path? Try, maybe fail, but do it on your terms, in line with your values.

## Know it's your path

How do you recognize your own path and know when you're actually on it? You don't. Not entirely, anyway. Sometimes you can't see it clearly until much later.

I feel like I'm on my path when I'm doing work that matters – and what matters to me might not be important to someone else. But when I'm doing something valuable and I feel good about it, I can be fairly certain that I'm taking my best path and choosing my own adventure. It can definitely end up being the wrong path (leading to failure or dragons), but at least it's mine and I can course-correct.

When I'm on someone else's path, it feels like I'm simply trying to make someone else happy by doing work that means more to them than to me. That's okay sometimes, because we've all got bills to pay and life to manage, but I can't see any real enjoyment or sense of accomplishment in the long term.

We all want to do work that matters. Stick to your values, follow your true instincts and fulfillment can be a daily proposition.

# Just like everyone else

You're weird. I am too. It's because we're different. Being weird is really just being your honest, unique self.

What I mean by "weird" is unique or different, because no one is exactly the same as anyone else. So, being true to who we are can make us seem weird at times, even if we aren't weird. The more we try to fit in or blend in, the less authentic we tend to be. In this case, weird doesn't mean purple hair or clown noses; it's about being true to yourself. It might even be unnoticeable on the surface.

We've been taught in school or in corporate jobs that being unique isn't good. In order to be productive and useful members of society, we've got to fit in and be more like the rest of the world. Always be professional. Don't stand out too much.

Here's the rub, though. Everyone else is also weird, even if they pretend they're not.

In work, we try to mask our weirdness with professionalism (I hate this word). We can wear suits or grey skirts and use the latest marketing jargon. "Synergy!" "Viral!" "Conversion!" Be careful not to swear, get too excited or passionate, and definitely do not let your personality shine through.

If we don't let our weirdness rise to the surface, we don't let our work stand out.

## A yoga teacher factory

So many yoga teachers feel interchangeable. They all speak the same, use the same soft voices (men and women) and the same tired parables – even though there are thousands of traditional yoga stories to choose from. It seems like there's a factory that pumps out identical Yoga Teacher Bots™, all wearing the same stretchy pants.

I was drawn to Caren because she's different. In fact, I wanted to work with her even before she contacted me for a new website. You can't trade her for another yoga teacher. First, in all of her online teachings, she does each pose with her dog, Willow. Seriously, every single one. Secondly, she talks openly about her struggle with depression. Screw the fact that all yoga teachers are supposed to be enlightened and perfect (physically and mentally), Caren tells her real story.

Her openness about depression could potentially put people off. At least, that's a fear we'd have if we were in her shoes. But, I'm certain it doesn't turn anyone off. The opposite is true, because her openness actually shows her humanity. She stands out in a competitive industry by being her real, flawed self. Caren's "weirdness" (by yoga teacher standards) makes her a normal human being. And we like humans, since underneath all that professionalism, we're human, too.

## The difference between you & those you admire

In the beginning, you might fear that you won't be successful. Once you achieve some success, you might be afraid that you won't get any more. Once you have a lot of success, you might worry about letting down your now-sizable audience if you change anything or say the wrong thing. At any stage, there are always fears.

It's interesting how we often want to emulate others' successes but not emulate the fact that they probably achieved this success by being themselves. Their uniqueness is thought of as visionary or as radiating charisma – as if what makes them *them* was just a brilliant marketing strategy (think: Richard Branson).

But when we're starting out, we feel like being our honest self might put others off. Somehow the same logic I described above, if applied to us, doesn't seem to stick.

People are drawn to leaders because they're true to who they are and what they value. Their uniqueness is magnetic.

Being exactly like a high-profile leader won't guarantee success for the rest of us. So why not be exactly like yourself instead? Let your own weirdness be what differentiates your work. Being yourself can be so endearing and attractive to others.

So let's all be weird together. And no, I don't live in Portland.


## Professional profanity

I swear. At home, in meetings, and in my writing. Not all the time, not even that often, but enough that it's incredibly noticeable to some people. And occasionally I get called out on it.

So, why do I swear in business situations and in print? Doesn't it make me look bad? Uncreative? Belligerent? Unprofessional?

Typically, I swear to make a passionate point or plea or to call attention to something I think is important or disturbing or exciting. Cussing can make people listen, take notice, and feel an emotion (positive or negative).

I don't use profanity simply to make a point, though. I swear because I swear. That's who I am, and always have been. I am my brand, and my brand tends to preach about being yourself, regardless of the situation. I've always been a little bit of a troublemaker, and I'm okay with that. I make trouble not to be mean, but to make people question things they might otherwise take for granted.

I also don't believe in professionalism or being business-like, because even when it's well intentioned, it's phony. Pretending that your personality is something it's not, to make yourself look better (or even just to look proper), doesn't sit well with me. Obviously, there's judgment involved here, like avoiding the f-bomb with a children's group, but you're more than capable of making those calls.

What if we acted like genuine, real, flawed people to each other, in every situation? That sounds nice. If I watered down or censored myself, I wouldn't be honest with myself or with others.

I never swear, though, in reference to someone else—to put them down or to make them look bad. To me, that's distasteful and disrespectful. And while I don't value professionalism, I certainly believe in respect – especially online, where it's easy to run your mouth or be negative to others.

One time someone asked if I would swear in a meeting with car company executives. It was such a random scenario, but oddly enough, I had actually been in that situation a few times earlier in my career. I told him that I spoke the way I normally do, which probably included a few expletives. Both times I got the job.

In any situation, whether it's a meeting at a huge corporation or a coffee shop get-together with a fellow solo entrepreneur, I let my personality (with all its flaws) shine through. Especially in business situations, I'd rather the other party knows who I am as a person so we can see if we'll work well together. I'm human and so are they. There's no need to front.

A lot of people might think this attitude could threaten my business or decrease my perceived credibility, but at least in my case, it hasn't. I've been booked solid for years and I'm lucky enough to pick and choose my clients and collaborators. I believe this is partly because I'm upfront about who I am. My swearing does not reflect my work abilities or work ethic, just as being covered in tattoos doesn't make me a criminal – they just reflect my personality and inherent weirdness.

I completely understand if people find my use of profanity offensive or distasteful, because it's their right to have an opinion. But like me or lump me, I'm comfortable with who I am and how I come across. My worth comes from an internal source. I realize I'm not for everyone, and I'm completely happy with that.

## Learning vs. school

Just like swearing is part of who I am, so is the fact that I learn by doing, not being told how things are done. You might learn in a different way, and that's good, too. The best way to learn is however you learn best—if it's school, go to school. If it's life, get out there and experience everything you can.

I did well in high school, so the adults in my life said that I needed to go to university. I chose a tough program and got early acceptance. After one year, I realized I wasn't doing it for myself; I was doing it for others. I was there because I was *supposed* to be there – becoming that professional member of society who values himself based on his salary.

So I quit.

During school, I had started making websites for fun, around the time the Internet was starting to get a little mainstream. I built one website in particular, called pseudodictionary, that got really popular and was even featured in WIRED magazine. This side project led to my first web design job.

I hated the job right from the start. I never wanted to work for someone else or to follow a company that was guided by someone else's values. But I also didn't know the first thing about running a business.

I used that time to help the company grow – eventually becoming the creative director – and learn what I needed to make a business work: contracts, dealing with clients, setting timelines and budgets, that sort of thing.

There was an end game in sight, but I worked hard to get better at my craft and develop business skills, too. When I quit a few years later, I was in a better place to start a company than if I had launched right out of school. And the clients followed me.

I learned a lot of lessons (see: mistakes) when I started working for myself, but I minimized them by learning how someone else did it first. I couldn't have received that kind of education in school. I had to learn it first-hand.

## One million dollars

When I was young, around the time I was reading those *Choose Your Own Adventure* books, I wanted to make a million dollars a year when I started my own company. That was my goal. If I could reach that benchmark, I'd be successful. My worth would bust at the seams.

So, I started doing work focused on that financial target. It guided the decisions I made and led me down specific paths. I said yes to almost every project, worked over 80 hours a week and didn't do much else. But the million dollars a year dangled like a carrot in front of me.

The carrot remained until I realized that money was a horrible goal for me – not because I hated money (I don't), but because my goal had nothing to do with my values. The million dollars was just something I thought I *should* accomplish. It was a path set by others and I didn't like it. Once I realized that this was my own business and I could focus on whatever I wanted to do, I felt free.

Around that time, I was primarily creating websites for professional athletes. I would meet with them in person and I got tickets to see games all over North America. It was a great job for a pro sports fan.

The only problem was, I'm not interested in professional sports. I don't watch games, I don't follow players, and I don't understand the celebrity factor of many athletes. Designing sports websites definitely wasn't a path I was choosing for myself, or one that aligned with my values – or even one that felt useful for anything but earning a pay-cheque.

I realized that money wasn't a valid goal for me when I didn't feel more accomplished by getting more of it. Making lots of money didn't make me feel better. In fact, I was actually feeling worse, because I was working far too many hours and not living my life.

I was doing projects that I didn't care about, because they paid well, instead of sharing awesome work. I didn't feel like I could truly be proud of what I was doing and what I was putting out into the world.

Designing websites *just* for more income led me to realize that it's critical to care about what you do. A funny thing happens when you focus on work that you love; more soon starts to appear. Like attracts like. Plus, that intersection between enjoying what you do and getting paid to do it is the sweetest place of all.

## But money isn't evil

I've been told that in order to make work that truly matters, you have to distance yourself from money. Mixing art and money is apparently a recipe for disaster. This feels naïve, though, as if money is intrinsically bad. But what if the more money you make, the more good you can do in the world?

Money can be an enabler and it's definitely an amplifier. If you're focused on yourself, money will make you even more self-obsessed. If you're focused on others, money can enable you to help more people in need (think: Bill Gates and his foundation).

Money also makes a point. You can measure how much people value what you do by how many people will give you money for it. It sounds crass, but it's one of the best ways to gauge how much other people value your business. Make no mistake, this value has nothing to do with your own, intrinsic value, objectives, or sense of personal worth. But until money changes hands, other people aren't valuing the business you've built as much as when they're paying you for it.

People can value you as a person, or even value a hobby without a financial transaction, but if the work you're doing is a business, money needs to change hands (from theirs to yours).

## Jobs vs. hobbies

Just because money isn't my main goal, and making money isn't very high on my list of meaningful activities, it doesn't mean I don't see its many benefits. I've worked hard to be profitable since I started my company. I didn't want to invest much at the start, so I began as cheaply as I could (in my parents' basement, which is so stereotypical for a nerd).

If I was burning through more money than I was making, I'd quickly re-evaluate what I was doing. I never bought into the dot-com boom philosophy of "it takes money to make money." Instead, I believe in starting and staying as financially lean as possible and growing only when sales grow, too.

What I do is a job, even if that job is working for myself. If making websites were a hobby, I'd make them in my free time and not worry if I saw even a penny for my time. Jobs make money and hobbies cost money. I have lots of hobbies, and I think they're important to keep my brain refreshed, but no one can live on hobbies alone – unless your hobby is playing Dungeons and Dragons, in which case you can't live on that hobby alone, but you will definitely be living alone...

# When's enough?

Here's how I think about money: *when do I have enough?* It's an odd question for a business owner, but it has radically changed how I approach my job, my work and my life.

I got this question from a friend who's a contract accountant for a large Alberta corporation. While he technically works for himself, he's very much a money and numbers guy, focused on practical details.

We were out surfing one day when he brought up the notion of making enough money for the year. He explained that he accepts all the projects he can without burning out, until he's made enough to cover his basic necessities for the year and save for retirement.

Once he meets that target, he doesn't take on any more work and travels to surf, climb and go on adventures. When he hits his "enough" amount, he closes the computer and walks away for a while—sometimes 5 to 6 months at a time.

This approach stuck with me instantly because I had never heard of someone saying they'd made enough money. Most business owners are focused on constant growth. We're always so caught up in the "more" of money, we don't tend to ask additional questions. We also tend to focus on the bottom end of money: is there enough to pay rent and feed myself and my family? But what if we hit the upper end? Do we really need more? Does the upper end need to be so far into the sky or can it be enough to live a simple life?

I figured out my upper target a few years ago. Once I hit that mark, I don't need to work for a while and can focus on writing, music or whatever I like. I live very frugally (I'd call myself a minimalist if I was cooler, but instead I'm just a cheap bastard) and because my work is virtual, I don't have much overhead or many business expenses. I also have an automated savings account to put money away for later.

Knowing what's enough enables me to travel with my wife for 2-3 months a year, on average. It's also why I can take large chunks of time off to explore new ideas and experiments. Neither my friend nor I are the type of people who would hit that mark and then sit on the couch watching soap operas. Instead, it frees us up to pursue hobbies, side projects and other interests. And sometimes those side projects turn into additional sources of income (shameless plug: this is probably the topic of my next book).

The "enough" mark creates freedom. Once it's hit, we both have the freedom to choose new adventures and explore fresh ideas and places.

## No goals

Once I abandoned my million-dollar goal, I realized I didn't have a replacement strategy. In fact, I didn't even know what an actual business plan entailed. I still don't.

At first, I thought I could fix my sudden lack of direction by finding better goals. Try as I might, I couldn't think of anything that made sense. Did I want 100 employees? Definitely not. I've never wanted to manage people. Did I want investors and growth? No, because that would make me feel like I was working for someone else. Did I want to make a name for myself in the design industry? Nope, I'd rather just do my work and share it with anyone who's interested, designers or not.

So, I decided not to have any goals. Not a single one. Not then, not now. I still avoid them as much as possible, almost as much as I resist owning a suit and tie.

This might seem like a total slacker mentality, but a lack of goals isn't the same as a lack of passion and drive. Where I lack in goals, I hold true to my values and let them guide my business – and I work hard at sticking to them.

I see goals as binding and limiting. They lead you in a single direction with a single focus. You have to pick path A instead of path B, because path A leads you to the goal in a shorter distance. Once you're pointed at a goal, you don't have much choice about the path you take. That's why I took on every project that came my way when I wanted to make a million dollars a year.

Now I let my values guide me, because they provide more freedom of choice. If I value doing good things and helping others, there are literally millions of ways to make that happen. I can pick the path I want and stay true to those values. They're vague enough not to impose limits, but clear enough to guide me in the right direction.

Letting values guide my work is freeing. It means that if given the opportunity, I can always choose freedom over money. Obviously this can't always be the case, since we don't live in a perfect world, with tiny little helper elves doing all the dirty work (and baking us cookies). This is why work is called "work" and not "super happy fun time." Bills need paying, clients can be stressful and sometimes the small tasks seem meaningless if we lose track of the bigger picture. But as long as our values primarily take the lead, it's okay.

Being guided by values also enables me to try and fail with impunity. If I try to reach a goal and don't achieve it, I've failed to reach that goal. If I stay true to my values and fail, I've still upheld my beliefs. I just need to try something else, try in a different way, or try again at a later time. Either way, I've never compromised my values; I just need to change things up and pick a different path, otherwise I'll get stuck in an endless loop, continually failing to slay that dragon.

## Start by stopping

Sometimes you need to walk away from a situation to really figure it out. There's better perspective when you remove yourself and examine it from another angle.

I could keep doing the exact same thing with my business for months and years and even decades. It's profitable and I enjoy it. But this heads-down approach won't work forever, because it doesn't leave any time to check in and see if my path aligns with my principles. Challenging myself and pushing against my fears are two of my core values, and that won't happen if I'm endlessly building client websites. If I don't try new things and new directions, I feel like I'll stagnate.

Recently, I came face to face with this situation and realized that I had to walk away for a while. I needed to forget about my work for a bit so I could examine it with a fresh perspective.

I was scared to hit the pause button, because nothing was technically broken and mostly, because change is scary. What if I changed things and ended up with zero clients? What if I ruined a perfectly successful business by experimenting with ideas that didn't work?

Walking away temporarily forced me to think about what my business means and how I can better help my clients.

After taking a break from the problems that lacked solutions, a funny thing happened: the answers were quickly and clearly evident. I rebuilt my practices and processes to better serve me *and* my clients.

Meaningful work is like a drug – and just like drugs, you eventually become immune to their effects and need to up the dosage just to the feel the same high. I needed to up my meaningful work dosage.

Sometimes, in order to stay true to yourself and your values, you need to innovate through change. And sometimes that means stopping and stepping back for a while.


## Start immediately

Choosing a path implies action. A choice is a starting line, so make a decision to begin right there – then make sure you finish, because starting without finishing is the same as not choosing. You need to eventually figure out if what you started and finished actually works by putting it out there. It can be scary, but you need to turn that page and keep going.

It's easy to get caught up in all the reasons not to start. It feels safe not to stick your neck out and do the work you want to do. Why test the waters when they might be cold and you can stay on dry land?

Most reasons to delay are invalid if you get right to the core: no time, no money, no audience. These are all future concerns, which make it hard to start anything. Worry about those things later or not at all. Make small decisions at first, and start moving in a direction that feels right.

There's no path if you aren't moving. It's just a single point in the road. The view might be great, but stasis never changed the world (or bought a yacht). The only way to see if your work might have traction is to do it and put it out there.

Clearly, there are times when we need to walk away, or take a break or even change things up. I know that first-hand. But needing a change shouldn't be an excuse for not starting at all. If you try something and need to take a break from it, that's one thing. If you think about starting something but don't try it, that's another problem altogether.

Start now. No excuses.

# BOOK TWO

# Overcoming obstacles on your path to adventure

*"There are only two mistakes one can make along the road to truth;*

*not going all the way, and not starting."*

Gautama Buddha

## The future isn't now

Going your own way, down a path no one has ever forged, is scary territory. It's not enough to be curious and to be yourself; you've actually got to do real work. It's easy to get tripped up or overwhelmed with questions like, "What do I do next?" or "What happens if?" when all that matters is, "Where do I start?" So let's do exactly that, and start dealing with some of the trickiest issues you'll face along the way.

Sometimes, we get ahead of ourselves before we even begin. We start thinking about next steps, five years down the road, what-ifs, or how it could all fail at a later date.

We focus on the future, which hasn't happened yet, and we have no way of predicting. This cuts into focusing on the present and actually starting something. We turn our attention not to our work, but on what could come from it.

This is another reason goals can be a hindrance. A goal implies something will happen in the future. It takes us away from the present and can even stop us from doing the work, since what if it fails? Why even try? Why put it out there? What if no one likes it?

Focusing on the present requires real effort. It means not checking Twitter or email every five minutes or daydreaming about being interviewed on every huge podcast. It means doing what's required, right now – and success still isn't guaranteed. But if you don't do the work, nothing will change, so why not at least try?

For good or for bad, you aren't entitled to the results; you're only entitled to do the work.

Our egos make it hard to let go of potential outcomes, but it's important to forget the future. Entitlement is ugly and quickly turns people off. The results of your effort — fame, money, power, etc. – will either appear or they won't. Spending even a second thinking about tomorrow requires you to stop thinking about the work you should be doing today. The results might not happen. But if what you do aligns with your values, those results won't matter. The fact that you went all-in will be enough. And if the labour itself isn't enough, perhaps you need to switch up what you're doing.

Spend your time worrying about what's now, not what's next. It's the only way to ensure you do meaningful work regardless of an outcome you can't predict or set.

## There's no time

Thinking there's no time is one of our biggest excuses. If you work a full-time job, have children, and do too much as it is, how can you find the time to write that book, launch your own business, paint a masterpiece, or anything else?

We're all busy. We work long hours and feel like there's not even enough time to sleep properly. But pursuing meaningful work isn't about magically finding extra hours in the day; it's about prioritizing the time we've all got.

What if instead of reading, you wrote? Instead of watching TV, you made videos? Instead of listening to music, you learned how to play guitar?

It takes sacrifice to make something great. In order to shift your mindset and experiment with ideas, you have to choose a new path. You have to change your paradigm from consumption to creation. Then the possibilities are limitless.

Once you choose a path toward creativity, it becomes easier to prioritize. Why watch TV when there's important work to be done? Why get caught in a social media time warp when there are great ideas to develop?

If there's something creative or innovative inside you that needs to come out, get to work and start now.

## Work is sacrifice

In a presentation at the *beyond tellerrand 2013* conference, graphic designer James Victore described how he was almost evicted after spending his rent money to print and hang posters that offered a different take on Columbus Day. Everything has a cost involved, and all good work requires some sacrifice. He sacrificed his rent because his work had a message that he couldn't stop himself from sharing.

Victore paid for the freedom to express his art. His work is now in the MoMA – and he probably has less trouble paying rent.

His speech to a group of young designers explained why he puts everything on the line to create meaningful work. A person in the back row (it's always a person in the back row) asked why he didn't value life's necessities. James replied that he did, but he didn't want his gravestone to say, "Here lies James. He paid his rent."

Every time you do one task, you're choosing not to do something else. If you truly value the work you create, choose to do it. There's no way to do everything and still keep your whole life in balance. Most artists and creators only know the word "balance" as a concept. Choosing to work on what you value means not choosing something else. This is okay.

What are you willing to sacrifice in order to make great and meaningful work? It doesn't have to be your rent money, but we're all busy, tired, stressed and being pulled in several directions. What can you cut out to create room for making something great?

## Money to start

Money tends to be another factor that keeps us from starting or doing the work we want to do. "If only I had enough money, " we think, "then I could start the business I've always dreamed about."

You can start without money. Scale the idea back to its essence and think of it as a prototype. What is your work? Without even knowing what it is specifically, I would guess that it helps someone else to solve a problem. If you want to be a web designer, you'd help people by making their websites. If you want to own a car dealership, you'd help people find cars.

Making your work about helping people doesn't mean giving away websites or even cars, but it can mean giving advice about either (or both, if it's a website for a car dealership). Help people for free, as often as possible, without expecting anything in return. Tell them honestly why one car is more suited for them or one idea for a website is better than another. This isn't charity work; it's just a way to slightly reframe your work.

If you have a message or story that will inspire or entertain people— tell it. You don't need a book deal or a film contract; you can simply set up a free blog and tell your story. Worry about selling it later. No creator was ever punished for telling too much of their story or giving too much of it away freely.

If you think your idea is too big to start without funding or a full-time commitment, you're thinking too far ahead of yourself. Scale the idea back to its core and start immediately.

Ideas and work can be small in the beginning, and they don't have to emerge as full-fledged businesses. Start while you're working full-time somewhere else, if necessary. Start with as much or as little time as you've got. But start.

## Side projects are experiments

Nathan Barry taught himself to code by creating and selling his first iPhone app, just after his wife had a baby and while he still had a full-time job.

The book he later wrote about creating that app sold more than $12,000 on its release day. Nathan's also gone on to create an email capture web application, write more books, and make a few more iPhone apps. He didn't quit his day job until he had established several income sources from those side projects

Nathan started all of these projects with little to no money, all while raising a new family. He's now scaled all of these "experiments" into full-time businesses.

I also created my first book with almost no money. I bartered, traded and borrowed nearly everything I needed. I made the book digital-only to avoid inventory and to ensure I didn't go into debt or borrow from my existing business to publish it. Once I made some money with that book, I used it to write and pay for services to make another. Then I used the money from that to create another, bigger book.

If I had focused on where I wanted my writing to go or what I dreamed my writing could be, I may have quit doing web design and focused on writing full-time (probably in a cabin in the woods somewhere). I may have printed thousands of copies that would still be sitting in my office. They might have sold, or they might not have, but that's not the point.

Starting incrementally made it easy for me to transition into more writing, as writing incrementally shifted from a side project to a larger amount of work.

# A wooden puzzle

One summer, I was at a coffee shop (more a shack, actually) in a town comprised of four buildings. While the owner was making my coffee, I noticed a bunch of wooden puzzles, the kind where you have to put the pieces together so they all fit back into the box – almost like 3D Tetris. Done incorrectly, the pieces don't fit and the box won't close.

I immediately got to work on the puzzle by trying to fit two pieces together. Then I added another, then another until I got something that almost fit into the original box. Except it didn't. It was off by a few pieces. So, I had to try again, which I did until I got it to fit.

If I had tried just that one time, I would have failed and stayed a failure at the puzzle box. If I had tried the first two or three times, I still would have failed at it.

It was only because I tried and failed (until I didn't fail) that I successfully got the pieces back into the box. It didn't work at all, until it did. All I had to do was keep experimenting with different possibilities – making choices and moving forward in the adventure.

# Being afraid to die

Our fear of failure often prevents us from attempting things. It feels safe not to try, but not trying is the only way you're guaranteed to fail. Don't fail in advance by not even making an attempt.

With something as silly as a wooden puzzle, few of us would be afraid to try. The stakes for winning or losing are so low that neither truly matters. But when it comes to our art, our ideas, and our work, there's much more involved, and sometimes we feel that fear of trying.

But what if our greatest fears about that work came true? Would we die? Would it be impossible to try anything again? Would we be unable to start again?

Most of the time, our fears come down to being judged by others. And it's a valid fear, because other people can be really fucking judgmental. Letting that judgment actually stop you from doing something, though, only hurts you. Know that everyone else (including the most successful people in the world) is judged, too. In fact, wildly successful people are judged exponentially – every day. But they push on. We need to do the same. Pushing past the fear of being judged and doing the work is exactly what can lead to *great* work.

Don't let the fear of being wrong give you decision paralysis, either. You could have two paths and they could both be wrong. Or both be right. Go anyway and risk being wrong. You won't know until you try and if you are wrong, you can go back and pick a different way.

Unfortunately, this fear of failing won't go away. Everyone's got it. The best you can do is realize it's part of being human and push through anyway. Letting fear hold you back is really just failing yourself and your potential.

## Grateful fears

I got an email from a mailing list subscriber who read my thoughts about fear and my list of everything that scared me. She, too, had written a similar list of her fears.

But then she realized that everything she was afraid to lose was something she was grateful to have. She was afraid of losing her husband, because he was one of the most important people in her life, and afraid of getting sick, because she had always been healthy.

That's an awesome way to look at things. Fear is losing what you might already be grateful for having, so let gratitude shine through that kind of fear.

Remember that taking a chance is exactly what can lead to this sense of gratitude. My reader wouldn't have her husband, for example, if they hadn't risked dating and getting married (which is definitely scary stuff). If you weren't afraid of anything, you'd have nothing of value to lose. So turn your fear into gratitude. Be happy that it's there, because it means you've got something worth losing.

## Acknowledge, then do

I'm grateful for the business I've built, so I'm afraid that if I rock the boat and try new or innovative things, I'll lose everything I've worked so hard to create. I'm grateful for my audience, so I'm afraid I'll lose it whenever I hit "publish" on an article or newsletter, or release a book.

I handle this fear by acknowledging that I'm afraid, then doing it any way. That can obviously lead to some epically stupid decisions, and I always have a steady stream of people who unsubscribe, unfollow and don't want to hear what I have to say, but pushing past my fear of sharing has also led to huge and new opportunities. Sharing my ideas is a risk I'm always willing to take.

I'm okay with either sharing the stupidest or the smartest ideas—because they're my ideas. And I know more ideas are always on the way.

## Courage creates possibility

My friend Matt was recently at a coffee shop in Nashville and realized that Jason Mraz (a famous pop singer-songwriter) was sitting nearby. Matt's a fan, so it made him giddy like a small child to know that someone he respected so much was just a few feet away.

After a few minutes of working up the courage, Matt went over, said hello and shook Jason's hand.

Then Jason did something Matt didn't expect. He asked Matt's name and invited him to sit down and chat, like normal human beings. So they spent a few minutes talking music, Nashville and craft beer.

Matt was fearful about talking to someone he looked up to, but went ahead anyway, and now he has a pretty fun story about that time he met Jason Mraz in a Nashville coffee shop and chatted about craft beer.

The only way to push past fear is to acknowledge it and fight through it with first-hand experiments. Sometimes the results can be pleasantly surprising.

By the way, this technique works not just for small stuff like talking to Jason Mraz, but for pretty much anything you might be afraid to do. Fear, acknowledge, and most importantly, do.

## Does fear even exist?

Fear plays you against yourself. It can't actually do anything to hurt you, but it makes you think that it's the biggest, baddest bully in the playground, ready to slap you down if you stand out too much.

Fear only has the strength you give it. Its power lies in making you too afraid to try something. So if you're afraid but try something anyway, fear loses its power.

I'm afraid of almost everything: leaving my house, groups of people, heights, flying, sharing my writing, being criticized, talking to people, just to name a small few. And if there's something I'm not aware that I fear and you ask if I'm afraid of it, I'll probably develop a new fear right there on the spot.

One time I wrote down all my main fears. It was a big list. Only one or two of them had the potential to result in my death, and both of those weren't very probable situations, like being eaten by a bear. The rest would, at worst, bruise my ego and make me look bad.

I face my fears and push toward them every time. I continue to leave my house, exist in groups of people, write and publish things. I keep trying to innovate, create new things, and stretch my limits.

I start small at first, with small pushes. I know that being afraid and moving forward don't have to be mutually exclusive. I work up to medium pushes. Fear still can't do anything if I don't give it any power. Then I push harder. Don't worry; fear can take it, and fear can't fight back.

*push*, Push, **PUSH**.

# Being afraid in public

I've been a touring musician as long as I've been a web designer, which seems odd to most people, given how introverted I am. I'm awkward in groups, I'm not comfortable out in public, let alone on stage, and I have a hard time communicating verbally. Seems like a recipe for disaster or failure, right? Playing shows, on stage, in front of others—sometimes lots of others.

But I started small, with small pushes against the fear of being on stage and sharing the music I write. I would sit in a park with the people in my band, not playing for people per se, but playing music around other people.

When I conquered that and didn't actually die, I moved up to open mics, where every other person in the room was equally scared to perform (at most open mics, you're usually playing for other musicians).

From there, my bands booked shows at smaller clubs and played for handfuls of people (if we were lucky). And still, I didn't die. People listened and some even bought CDs or t-shirts. Or better yet, some people came to more than one show – which I've always thought was the best compliment you can give a band.

I moved on to playing bigger shows sometimes, and even touring Canada and the US, playing almost every night. I've never become less afraid of being on stage, talking into a mic, or interacting with crowds, but over time I definitely learned to see the fear, acknowledge it, and then walk out onto the stage anyway. I've played wrong notes and didn't die. I've played the wrong parts at the wrong times and not been laughed off stage. Most of the time people don't even notice those tiny mistakes.

Sometimes the shows where I felt the most self-conscious were the same ones where lots of people told me afterward just how much they enjoyed it.

I wouldn't have experienced any of this if I hadn't started experimenting with my fears.

# Why pushing is important

I'm motivated by seeing how far I can push myself – how far I can take my experiments and how close I can get to actually knowing who I am, or how far I can go with any of my ideas. I'm not satisfied with anything, ever, so I feel like I need to keep stretching or I'll die a stagnant, uncreative death. My tombstone will read: "Here lies Paul. He didn't do a whole lot." Even worse, it'll be carved in some horrible typeface (like Comic Sans or Papyrus).

I think experimenting with fear is important, because it makes us present and accountable to ourselves, and it ensures we live meaningful lives by learning how much we're capable of accomplishing. We have no idea what we can really do unless we try things and challenge our perceived limits.

Confronting fear can also create some of your proudest moments. I feel good about myself if I do something I was scared to do. Almost everything I've feared has turned into something I can't believe I was ever scared to try.

# Out there, in the distance

Why push against fears? Why move toward them if it makes us uncomfortable? Isn't it nice to stay unafraid but safe?

Only by experimenting with fear can we find our true limits – not the limits we think we have, because these are only assumptions until we try. When we push up against fear, we realize that our limits are much further away than we realized; sometimes those limits are so distant, we can't even see them.

Run with dangerous ideas. Great work requires great risk. Achieving something doesn't come from a lack of fear; it comes from being afraid and trying anyway. True courage typically involves a great deal of fear, but it also means proceeding anyway.

Start running (but not with scissors).

# The paradox of missing out

The more you worry about missing out on things, the more of your actual life is consumed by worrying about what you're missing. Constantly checking in on virtual activities means you're peripherally participating in everything, without actually participating in anything. It takes you out of being present and puts you into observing someone else who is only partially present.

Social media is a great example of FOMO (fear of missing out). The more we refresh our streams, the less we're actually doing anything. So, our work suffers because we think we might miss something that someone else says, does or posts.

The less time you spend catching up on what you think you're missing out on, the more time you can actually live your life, do your work, or connect with others in a present way.

## Flaws of perfection

School teaches us that failure is bad. If we fail at what we try in a classroom, we typically fail the class. There are no rewards for breaking boundaries, experimenting or exploring new paths.

This black-and-white approach closes off opportunities. It also doesn't equip us for dealing with a crazy, complicated real world where boundaries need to be pushed and experiments need to be done in order to make meaningful work.

Trying to be perfect prevents us from discovering our weaknesses and building on them. Trying to be perfect doesn't push anything, nor does it expose who we really are. Because we're not perfect.

Thomas Edison tried to create a sustainable and affordable light bulb many times before he actually made one that worked. If he hadn't experimented and failed hundreds of times, we wouldn't know his name. Einstein wrote thousands of research papers and most were considered either awful or simply average. It wasn't until he had tried several ideas and explored many new paths that he finally came upon his genius.

There's no innovator, inventor or creator in the history of the world who does something amazing without failing at least several times first. Failure is a requirement for success, so don't shy away from it. Instead, embrace failure as a stepping stone to greatness.

## Practice makes closer

Perfection is a myth, so practice can never make perfect. In fact, all that striving for perfection can actually lead you away from launching anything. The path to perfection makes it almost impossible to get your work out the door, because nothing will ever be perfect. Focus instead on great *enough* to launch and perfect *enough* for your audience to enjoy.

The book won't get finished if you're focused on making every sentence a timeless quotation for the masses. The painting won't get done if every square inch needs to be Louvre-worthy. Your work can be great enough.

Great enough means you've sweated out every bit of inspiration possible. Great enough means you've left it all on the stage. Great enough means you can push your work to the finish line.

Great enough isn't settling; it's launching.

So practice doesn't make perfect. Practice makes closer. Every time you work at what you do, you're one step closer to the next step. A whole bunch of these steps add up to launching.

Sometimes practice leads to failure and you have to abandon the work. In that case, try new variables or even try new work. Only more practice can lead you closer to success.

# Judgy

Fear can also make us afraid of what others will think. It's not that people might judge you; they will judge you.

I deal with this fear by showing up to it as often as possible. If I'm afraid of writing, I write. If I'm afraid that I'm not a strong enough web designer, I make more websites.

Action is the only difference between someone who constantly creates and shows off their work and someone who doesn't. Both people were afraid. Neither of them knew what the outcome would be. Neither knew how others would judge them, but the first person did it anyway.

So why are you afraid of being yourself? What have you *really* got to lose?

# Every single time

Whenever I send out an email to my mailing list, I lose subscribers. Whenever I tweet, I lose at least one follower. Whenever I write a book or an article, I get at least a few scathing reviews, pointing out flawed logic, a lack of skill or an easily refutable point.

People email me about what I design or write and tell me that my work is awful or that my ideas are bad. I get at least one negative email, tweet or review every week. One time someone gave me a 1-star (out of 5) review for my cookbook because, "it was good, but not *War & Peace* good."

Maybe it's because I like to push buttons or write about stealing ideas and swearing in meetings. Maybe it's because I try to write in an honest voice that doesn't resonate for some readers.

So why bother putting work out into the world when I get figuratively slapped every time? I do it because I enjoy sharing who I am. I like connecting with people who like connecting with me (which is a small subset of the general population).

I'm not too bothered with unsubscribes or unfollows or rude emails. I just swear at my computer screen and quickly move on.

I don't remember the last time a negative comment or piece of feedback actually kept me up at night or ruined a whole day. As long as I'm aligned with my values and being honest with myself about what I share, I keep sharing. I share because even if some people hate it, some don't. And those people who don't are the ones I want to connect with and help through my work.

I'm not trying to please everyone all the time. I'm not even trying to please the people who like me all the time. We all have different values and even if they mostly line up, sometimes they don't, and that's okay. I'd rather focus on what I want to say and not how it might offend someone.

## What if

Meg is a health coach who helps people struggling with food issues and teaches them how to make healthier choices. There are lots of health coaches out there and just like yoga teachers, they tend to have an agreed-upon language and approved tone. But none of these coaches have Meg's story, and she's not interested in posturing or putting on airs. She doesn't care about being a good little Health Coach Bot™.

Before she became a coach, Meg spent two years in federal prison for dealing drugs. You can read about it on her business website. It's right there, for the whole world to see.

At first Meg was afraid to connect with her audience in her own way – an audience that wanted to learn about food and health, but not in the same way most other health coaches were communicating. But she thought, "what if?" What if she was just honest in how she talked about her business? What if she was honest about her story, so her audience didn't find out elsewhere, which could be awkward?

Meg went from fear to experimentation into grace. The grace of doing work her way. The grace of loving life and doing a job that is both rewarding and also pays the bills.

She began finding her voice in small steps. She added tiny bits of bravery to every post she wrote and to everything she did, until those little bits of bravery added up to a business that told her true story and aligned with her values.

She's now shopping her unique story to literary agents.

## Crisis of confidence

Most days when I'm writing, I wake up with a huge knot in my stomach. What if what I write isn't as popular as my last post or book? What if people finally figure out that I don't know anything?

What if no one buys my books, or worse, everyone who does wants a refund? What if that knock at the door really is the Creative Police?

These are scary thoughts, but they won't kill me or make it impossible to try again or to try something new. At worst, failure would bruise my ego (and my ego can take a gentle beating).

I wake up thinking about all these things and then I get to down writing. Being afraid of everything means being very afraid of the big stuff. There are too many unknowns, too many variables, and too much of me involved if it fails.

The only way I know how to proceed, though, is to keep going. Try, adapt, learn. Experiment first-hand.

I have a crisis of confidence every time I see a blank page. But then I start writing. And each word is a small push against that fear. I'm fighting it as I write this sentence, and if you're reading it, I've pushed against my fear of publishing what I write, too.

# Show up

If you frequently show up to your fear, you'll learn how to see it, acknowledge it, and then do what you're afraid to do anyway. You have to show up, probably every day – and especially if you don't want to or aren't feeling inspired.

Showing up and doing your work when you don't feel inspired sounds, well, uninspiring. And that's okay, because inspiration is bullshit. Everyone I know who's good at what they do isn't good because they have magic fairy dust or shoot unicorns out their ass. They're good because they do what they do as often as possible.

To become a better writer, I write around 500 words a day. To become a better designer, I design every time I'm hired to do a project. Sometimes it's awful stuff, things I wouldn't share with anyone. But sometimes what I write is worth sharing. If I work for long enough, my designs get to a place where I'm happy enough to share them with my clients. I increase my odds of doing better work by tackling it every single day. And sometimes when I don't feel like creating and do it anyway, I produce my best stuff.

My best work wouldn't exist unless I showed up and did it as often as possible.

# Tiny pieces

My job as a web designer requires me to be "creative on demand." There are always deadlines and deliverables, so I need to develop original assets for every project I'm hired to do. Even if I'm not feeling inspired or creative on a particular day, I still sit down and do the work.

I start small on those days, maybe by picking a typeface. Then I choose which colours are best suited for the project. Next, I put the colours and fonts together to see how they interact, and play around with different sizes and styles for headings and paragraph content.

Breaking my work into tiny pieces makes it feel less like a huge creative job and more like small tasks that I can accomplish – even if the muse isn't sitting on my shoulder. I start with tiny pieces and build from there, until what's left is a finished piece of work.

It's amazing how often this tactic succeeds and how much easier it is to approach work, especially creative work, when you break it into the smallest of tasks. It feels less daunting, like you don't have to twiddle your thumbs and wait for inspiration lightning to strike.

## The value of criticism

Your work shouldn't be so precious that it can't stand up to criticism. If it is, you should probably hold it close and not share it (there's value in creating work like this too—work that's just for you). But if your work is meant to be shared with the world, know that it will face criticism.

Feedback can only make you stronger. You need to be able to defend your ideas to see how they hold up to deeper investigation and provide value for others. Untested views are seldom worth holding, so facing a little criticism can only make your work stronger.

It's not easy, but most of the time, we need to separate our emotions from feedback on our work. I've had to do this for almost two decades now and face clients who may or may not like the ideas I present to them.

I can do a website mockup that I feel is the best mockup ever. I can spend hours working on my client pitch to ensure they buy in and want to use it for their business. But sometimes, it still doesn't work for them and I have to scrap it and start from scratch.

If I got angry, offended or upset every time this happened, I'd spend too many days unable to focus. Instead, the criticism shows that my work didn't provide as much value as it could, so I move on and try again. Yes, sometimes it sucks to work hard on something creative only to see it shot down, but I've never once dwelled on it for more than a few minutes.

If my work was so precious that it couldn't stand up to constructive criticism and feedback, I wouldn't be able to do it as a job.

## A (fall out of) love note

Listen to constructive feedback but ignore your inner critic. Fall of out of love with it immediately, because it doesn't serve you. The world needs you to create, not to constantly edit what you make and dwell on your perceived shortcomings.

We need you. Not the *you* that you're supposed to be, not the *you* that you think we want you to be, but *the real you*. The *you* that scares us a little because it's so honest (and even a little weird).

Being the real you is important, because it makes it easier to align yourself with your values and easier to keep doing meaningful work.

When the filters and masks are taken away, what's left is unique and magnetic.

You can't wait until later to do this. You can't wait until you've "made it" to show the real you. You owe it to yourself to start being you right now.

We love dwelling on our shortcomings because it's easier and less vulnerable than sharing our work with the world. It's safer to make something and simply say, "This isn't good enough" and hide it away. But, that deprives the world of our point of view and something that could make a real difference for someone else.

Fall out of love with your inner critic immediately. Kill its voice before it kills you.

## Vulnerability is courage

If you look up the word "vulnerability" in a dictionary, it sounds like an awful thing to be.

Definitions range from "susceptible to being wounded or hurt, as by a weapon" to "open to attack or assault" to "capable of being emotionally wounded." Those sound like horrible things. No wonder we avoid it.

If you remove the negative potential outcomes from the definitions (stop jumping to conclusions, Webster's!) then vulnerability is really just exposure. It's exposing yourself to emotions, to other people, to uncertainty, to risk. It requires showing up and sticking your neck out when you aren't sure of what comes next.

Why would we do this? Why would we leave ourselves that open, since it can lead to failure, ridicule or any myriad of bad things, probably involving weapons? There's no guarantee anything good will come of being vulnerable. So why bother?

Our society typically sees vulnerability as a form of weakness. Most of us think that strong people can't be so open. But in fact, the opposite is true.

In order to be courageous, we must first take a risk without knowing the outcome. Being vulnerable is what drives us to make leaps, start new ventures, and most importantly, make and own our choices. A willingness to try new things is our greatest measure of bravery, because we have to open up and see what happens.

In others, it's easier to see how vulnerability might be strength. We admire vulnerable people because they take the risks we wish we could take. But when we focus the lens back on ourselves, we feel that social perception of weakness.

*If I'm open and I fail, then people will think less of me.*

We think that risk and courage are so much easier for others, or we rest in the safety of thinking (or writing!) about vulnerability, instead of actually putting it into practice in our own lives.

Dr. Brené Brown (watch her 2010 TED talk) has studied vulnerability for over a decade. One of the key findings in her vast body of research is that there isn't a single instance of bravery that doesn't also require vulnerability.

The more we understand the connection between the two, the more we can realize that they aren't opposites.

**To have courage is to be vulnerable.**

Putting ourselves out there, despite knowing that if we do it enough we'll eventually fail (or fail right out of the gate), is a true and grand act of courage.

How will you be vulnerable today?

# It's all in how you frame things

I make things and share them with others. Sometimes it's books, photos or websites, and sometimes it's food. I try not to get caught up in labels, expectations or what will come from what I make. That's all in the future, and thinking about it before it happens does nothing but detract from my actual work.

A few years ago, I wrote a cookbook without knowing anything about writing a book, self-publishing, or even the most important part... cooking. I have no formal training, I'm not a chef, and I've never spent any time in a professional kitchen. I just wanted to create a book of great recipes, while answering people's questions about eating a plant-based diet. I didn't think of myself as a writer or a chef, and I still don't. I just like making things. And sometimes that thing is a vegan cookbook.

This perspective takes the pressure off. It eliminates the need to create a goal around what I'm making. It also makes success irrelevant, because I'm not a chef publishing a cookbook masterpiece, I'm just a guy who loves food and has some great recipes he wants to share. There's no way to fail, because I'm enjoying the entire process.

In the beginning, I didn't think too much about becoming a professional writer (which really means being paid for my writing). If I had, I might not have started, since that's a scary thought and a level of vulnerability I may not have embraced. What if my books flop? What if people say my blog posts are all wrong? Would I be good enough to be considered a real writer? I'm sure I couldn't have held myself up to the weight of that label. So, instead I just wrote.

If I live in the present while I create and don't worry about what happens once it's released into the public, then all I need to do is make sure the work aligns with my values.

If my values are to do good and help people, the cookbook is full of delicious food and will help anyone who wants to learn some new vegan recipes.

## Failure is an experiment

If you frame ideas as experiments, you can't technically fail at anything. You're just going to prove or disprove a theory you've arrived at through experimenting. And if it doesn't work the first time, you can iterate and try something different. It doesn't work until it does.

There's no formula that will ensure successful work. All you can do is generate ideas and test them. Succeed or fail, at least you've done the necessary work.

Persistence is the most important trait of successful people. Hardly anyone is successful right from the start. Most try, fail, try again, fail, try again. Their backstories are full of errors, almosts and rejections – until they're not. They picked up the puzzle box one more time. They kept choosing a new path until it led somewhere good.

If the result isn't what you intended or doesn't make you happy, you're now free. When you're working on an idea, you get caught up in making it work. There's vested interest in thinking, "I've come too far to fail now!" But if it does fail, lay all the puzzle pieces out and start from scratch. Try different pieces in unique ways. Go back to the start of the book and pick a new path. Avoid the dragon this time, since there's a road that bypasses him.

# How I experiment

**I focus on the task at hand, not the end result.** Focusing on the process allows serendipity and personal exploration to take over. Otherwise, I might inadvertently apply a subjective idea of how I want something to turn out, rather than what would be best for long-term discovery.

**I try not to create and judge at the same time.** Creation and judgment are very different thought processes and can interfere with each other, so they must be done separately. I experiment and explore every idea first (writing it down, drawing it out, actually trying to do it). Only then do I move into editing, curating, and judging to improve and refine the idea.

**I break the experiment down into the smallest tasks possible.** Then, I work completely on each small task. Only at the end do I tie all those tasks together. This prevents me from feeling overwhelmed or scared about tackling such a big project.

**I remember that these are experiments.** They're not full-time business ideas. First, I figure out how to run the experiment using the least resources possible. What is the core or essence of my idea that I can quickly prototype? Then I get that prototype in front of as many people as possible before pursuing it further. I fail fast.

**I don't repeat myself.** The same experiment can't have a different result unless I change the variables. If I experiment with an idea and it doesn't work, I either change things up or move onto a new idea. There's no point doing the same experiment over and over, hoping for something new to happen. If I want a different outcome, I have to change the experiment up a little — refocus for a new audience, try a different medium, or experiment with a completely new idea.

## Intentions are evident

Our intentions are always evident to others. We are mostly horrible liars, and sometimes, we're just lying to ourselves. Before starting any experiment, it's smart to evaluate why you want to do it in the first place. What are you trying to accomplish? How does this experiment align with your values?

As hipster as it might seem, the coffee industry has great examples of how business is shaped by intention. You can get a cup of coffee nearly anywhere—from gas stations to trendy local cafes to massive corporate chains and even most surf shops. Despite their shared business goal of staying profitable, they all have very different intentions.

Blue Bottle Coffee's mission statement talks about offering seats to the elderly on public transit and flossing daily. In contrast, Starbucks uses flowery corporate-speak to describe its high standards, ethics, and exceptional products. Can you guess where I'd rather have a coffee? Starbucks could be describing cars, computers or even social media. The lack of passion is evident and using flowery marketing language doesn't fool anyone.

Even people who haven't watched an episode of *Mad Men* can sense the intentions of these two coffee companies. Starbucks might spend lots of money to get their tone right, but they still feel like a business that's trying to sell you coffee. Blue Bottle, however, feels like people who love coffee so much, they want to sell you a cup that you'll love, too.

Our intentions are like a red ball shuffled around under three plastic cups. We like to think we're great magicians and we can trick our audience, but the cups are transparent to anyone playing the game.

Intentions explain why sales pitches sound like sales pitches, and why most commercials are immediately identifiable as commercials. We can innately understand what the other person really wants.

So why not pursue something good? That way, when people see your intentions, they'll feel good about them, instead of angry or disappointed.

When we put our own passion, humor, fear and love into our work, it means so much more and resonates more deeply with others. Why? Because it becomes a rallying point for ourselves and our audience. Think of it this way: a record label tells a band to write a song about a fictional girl named Jenny. The band releases that song to the world. Then the songwriter falls in love with a girl named Lisa and writes another song about her. They release this song, too. Which song do you think will make a stronger connection? Which song do you think will be more popular?

If your work is based on helping others, showing that intention is a no-brainer. People will be drawn to your work, because we're all a little selfish and want our pain to go away. But if your work is focused on making money, people will see that you want to relieve them of their hard-earned cash.

You can certainly try to chase things like money or fame or popularity; these things aren't wrong or even bad. But you'd better be the David-Fucking-Copperfield of what you do to hide those intentions. Otherwise, you've got to own them completely and openly (think: Donald Trump).

## No second-hand experiments

You could convince yourself that if someone already tried a certain path and failed, you don't need to try it, either. You see their failure as proof that the path leads nowhere.

But just as you can't take the same path to success as someone else, the same logic applies to failure.

You have to try for yourself to get valid results. To see what actually happens. You might be left with scars, but at least those scars will become visible reminders of your journey.

# How I validate an idea

I validate ideas by trying them out. Most of my initial ideas take almost no money and only require time to explore. If I enjoy doing the work, then the time is well spent.

I validate ideas by launching them – and every idea can be distilled down to something you can start with almost no money and some initial work. So, I start with the essence of the idea first, test it out with others, and see where it goes. Prototyping works.

Sometimes successful work can lead to less innovation, and then the real making stops. You become more like a factory production line than a meaningful creator.

Perfection is the biggest excuse for not launching. If only a few more things were perfect, we say, then it would be ready for other people to consume. If only we could just get this one piece right.

Perfection prevents launching because it's easy to keep circling back and endlessly refining. The truth is, perfection cannot even exist until it's tested, and even then, it's probably still impossible. Stop chasing perfection. Stop focusing on small details that don't matter and that hold you back from releasing big ideas.

## Super hero stuff

Helping people can lead to full-time work if enough people seek your help – and if you're in the business of helping people full-time? That sounds like the stuff of super heroes. You've proven that your prototype has legs. You can build on that success and start selling websites or cars.

When you're solving someone's problems with your valued expertise, you're going to satisfy a lot of people. They'll tell others how you helped them, and you'll have more people asking for help.

So help people. Start doing it right now

# BOOK THREE

# Art, craft & passion

*"Creativity is allowing yourself to make mistakes.*
*Art is knowing which ones to keep."*

Scott Adams

## Every entrepreneur is an artist

If you're doing your own work in your own way, you won't be happy with the status quo. Maybe you have an idea about how something could be smarter or work better. That's great; stir the pot a little more.

Doing your own work is important. Innovation comes from starting, saying, or trying something new – not from following what others have done or what worked for them. So be a rogue agent. Zig instead of zagging. This requires tremendous creativity, but thankfully you're showing up as often as possible to be creative.

# Craft & passion

I don't believe in "following your passion." I hate advice, and this is horrible advice. Passion is good, but it needs frequent examination. Is your passion motivated by external rewards (like fortune or fame) or guided by internal values that you feel at your core? Either way, passion isn't enough.

Instead, find your *intersection*—where what you do is meaningful and helps people who are willing to pay for your products or services.

It's not enough that you're excited about something; other people (your audience) also need to be excited enough to pay you for it. You could create a product so exciting that you let out childish "squees" every time you think about it. But if no one wants to buy it, you can't make a business from it.

Your intersection requires a great deal of craft. You have to be good at something. You can certainly be passionate about it, but you also have to be skilled. Otherwise, make it a hobby and enjoy it in your downtime. You never have to share your hobbies with anyone else or make them profitable, and this is the beauty of hobbies—they can be all about you.

If you aren't good at your craft yet, enough to make it into full-time work, ask yourself if you'd be willing to put in the time and sweat to become the best in the world. If yes, keep going. If no, find something else.

Once you've put in the time and sweat and you're still not closer to being the best, find something different—not everyone is good at everything and you haven't found your sweet spot yet, so you have to adapt. Experiment with new things. You don't have to be the best in the world, but you need to keep improving in noticeable ways.

Try to generate as many ideas as possible. Commit to developing them routinely and you'll eventually hit on one that you care about and are good at doing. Increase those odds by showing up often.

Passion is a tricky thing. You can be passionate about the process or the people involved in a project, for example, even if the work itself isn't the object of your obsession. You can be in love with the fundamentals but not the trappings, especially if it's in your intersection between craft and passion.

Find the intersection where your interests meet your skills and reach an audience that'll pay for your time, work, products or services.

# Craft vs. value

In 2007 I started a company with two friends. One is a programmer who now works at Twitter. The other is a marketing guy who has since started several successful companies. We all knew our respective crafts.

The company was an online ad network for environmentally friendly businesses (serving the ads on environmentally-focused blogs). It felt like the perfect idea. I've always been involved with eco charities, because stewarding the environment is something I care deeply about. So, building an eco-focused tech company aligned with my values and my expertise. We even tied charitable donations right into the business model, so as our revenues grew, so would our donations to environmental groups.

My co-founders were not only great friends, but also successful people (they still are). We had the best designs, solid code and a sound strategy to build an audience and consumer base for our product.

We took months to develop the perfect solution and get our audience excited about the launch. We had companies interested in putting their ads on our network, as well as high-traffic publishers and bloggers keen to feature "green only" ads on their sites.

But then September 2008 arrived and the global markets crashed. Advertising budgets, even if they weren't directly hit, shriveled up and died.

We were left with zero financial interest in our product. After trying for months to find new advertisers, we were forced to abandon the project. We had built what we felt was an incredible product that aligned perfectly with our values and passions. But in the end, we didn't have an audience willing or able to pay for it.

All three of us brought our skill and craft to the project, but the intended audience didn't see enough value or necessity to complete the transaction. Because the market crashed and changed, the business didn't have legs to stand on.

Sometimes having a refined craft is only a piece of the equation. You also need an audience ready to shell out cash in exchange for your work. My partners and I put in the work, but it ultimately failed because we couldn't convince the audience of its value in a tight economic climate.

# Connections are made between two people

Individuals, not the anonymous "masses," make connections with you. So don't bother trying to make everyone happy, or convince everyone to want what you make. It's impossible and it can quickly get disheartening to please people who don't care for it in the first place.

Your work is your story, told through your unique lens. Some will disagree with you, but some won't. Draw a line in the sand based on your values and stay true to what you believe. The people standing on your side of the line are now easier to pick out. They're your audience, allies, promoters and friends.

The only one who can make and share your work is you. It rests on your shoulders. It can be scary and overwhelming, but revolutions are necessary. Without them nothing would ever change and the world would be a pretty boring place.

The only way to really see if and how your work connects with people is to do it and then put it out there.

# Find your people

Your business is about *your* people. It's not just about you or what you make, but about everyone the work can touch. It's about their story and how they use what you've made – how something you make can help the whole group instead of just you.

Srinivas Rao calls these people your small army. These are the folks who find value in your work. They're the people who get what you're talking about. Most importantly, these are the people who show up to the work you create. They interact with it, buy it and even promote and share it.

These people are your royalty because they're willing to listen to what you have to say. These are the people who stand on your side once you've drawn that line in the sand. They show that you're not alone in what you do, and you show them the same.

Finding your people can be difficult, but it starts with a few questions: Who do you like to be around? How can your work help them? Who do you connect with naturally? Who feels closer to you, the more you share with them and reveal your honest thoughts?

Your people aren't necessarily those who follow you on social media. In fact, you might not even have a single interaction with most of them. They could be the 10 folks who bought your last piece of work. They are definitely your people if they told everyone they know about the work you do.

Your people don't have to be a huge group; they can just be that "small army." Connect with them individually at first and go from there. Help them if they need help, re-align what you do if it doesn't serve them anymore, and be as honest as possible with them at all times.

My people are on my mailing list. It's where I most enjoy communicating and interacting. It's a small group, for sure, but they're the people who are first to give me feedback, sign up for what I offer, and simply talk to me. I've spoken to dozens of subscribers on the phone and it only reinforced how much I enjoy interacting with them. I could lose my social media accounts tomorrow and not sweat it, but you'd have to pry my mailing list from my cold, dead, can't-connect-to-the-internet fingers.

## Rallying points

Do you remember in medieval times (me neither, but stick with me) when you were in battle, possibly losing or confused, and then someone would hoist up your flag?

You'd get the urge to fight just a little harder and move toward that flag, hopefully with more soldiers on your side doing the same.

The flag became a beacon that instantly identified a common cause. *Got to make it to my flag,* you'd think, and then you'd be surrounded by like minds (in this case, minds that didn't want to kill you). And from there, you could further your common goal.

The idea of flags as broadcast messages and rallying points is as old as culture.

Flags are more than just well-designed fabric with nice logos. They proclaim an immediately identifiable idea. What they stand for is more important than what they look like. You either believe it, and therefore stand behind it, or it doesn't resonate and you know it's not your flag. It's a black and white, cut and dried sort of thing.

In those old times, everyone wore basically the same suit of armor, so it was hard to tell who you should help and who you should use a sword against. Flags were used to differentiate the two.

Even now, it can still be hard to tell who's the right audience for your business, versus who most certainly isn't a good fit.

I like the idea of focusing your work around a "rallying point." It's more than simply branding, messaging or even business goals. It's a line in the sand, with your work and the values it represents on one side and everyone or everything else that doesn't fit on the other side. It immediately illustrates who's part of your small army.

It can be scary to draw that line in the sand – especially when it's *your* business. Doing so immediately alienates certain people or entire groups. But raising a flag is important because it acts as a beacon for those individuals who are your people, your tribe, and your audience. You hoist it up and they know where to find you.

What would a rallying point look like for a non-medieval business? Think of a corporate mission statement, like the lululemon manifesto. If you aren't into yoga, sweating and positivity, you won't like what it says – but then you wouldn't buy a pair of their pants anyway (unless you're into see-through pants). But if you do, you might read it and think, "HECK, YES. THIS" and you'd probably already be wearing their logo.

A rallying point doesn't need to be as specific as a manifesto, though. In my own business, it's really just defining how I feel about design, SEO and programming by writing lots of opinion pieces on my blog.

If someone wants to work with me, and then reads what I think about my industry and disagrees... they probably wouldn't have been the right fit and would make me want to pull my hair out.

But if someone finds me, digs what I have to say about what I do, and then we launch a project together—I guarantee it would at least start from common ground and understanding.

My logo has changed and even disappeared many times over the years, but what I stand for hasn't budged. I've always been about simple and direct design that serves individuals more than a metrics calculator.

Rallying points can simply be your values, expressed in some form of content—writing, videos, photography, etc. Or it can even just be the tone in which you communicate. It's whatever works to show your people that they are your people.

MailChimp's "Voice & Tone" website is a great example of non-promotional rallying content. It's not about one specific idea or value, but the company's manifesto comes through anyway. A rallying point can simply be how you communicate with people on a one-to-one basis.

The best marketing always takes a stand. It's not just about selling a product or service; it's about showing an audience why they should want it at any cost, simply because they agree with what you're doing. Chipotle's short film, "The Scarecrow," was less about burritos and more about why the company sells them.

Goals can be reached or adjusted if they aren't functioning, but rallying points align with the values and meaning behind what you do (not just the specifics of what you do). They're clear and noticeable and impossible to ignore. They're a bold statement that your work is more than the work, but also the reason why you're doing it in the first place.

So what's your rallying point? What does your flag look like when you raise it up – and who will be drawn toward it?

# Finish anything

When you have lots of ideas, it's hard to choose which ones to work on. Even more difficult, though, is to follow through and launch the ideas you start.

The beginning of any project is filled with passion and hard work. Everything seems amazing. You're exploring something fresh and new and it's tough to take your mind off all the novelty.

But then, inevitably, the passion fizzles out a bit. The work begins to actually feel like *work*. Maybe you even abandon the project, not in some grand gesture of deletion, but simply by working on it less and less until you forget it even existed.

I (mostly) avoid project burnout by doing a few key things that help me to stay focused and move quickly from idea to launch.

Before I explore an idea, I sit with it for a while. What are my intentions? What is guiding those intentions? Are they external or internal? If I can get past this phase, I figure out how to break the project into the smallest steps possible, so each individual task doesn't seem as daunting, or feel like I need divine inspiration just to continue.

I also like to reward myself for completing each small task. Maybe it's 10 minutes on social media to catch up with friends. Maybe it's a short yoga break in my lululemon pants.

During the project, I also like to think back to my initial intentions. It's good to refocus and remember the why, especially if you aren't feeling like you should proceed.

The most important part of finishing anything is saying no. If I'm working on an idea, I say "no" to almost everything: new projects, new clients, social engagements—basically anything that would take my focus away from what I'm doing. I take breaks, but there's a difference between breaks and things that cut into my ability to get the work done. I say no so I can say yes to what I'm currently doing – or I say yes to what I want to pursue.

If an idea truly isn't working, I might adapt the end result or my expectations, because maybe they weren't realistic. Maybe the audience doesn't see the value in what I've made. That's okay, because it was just an experiment. I can iterate and change up some variables or even walk away.

# Know when to quit

Sometimes our work doesn't work. Einstein said that trying the same experiment with the same variables and expecting different results is the definition of insanity. It's difficult to give up on a project, but sometimes it's necessary in order to make room for something new.

Frustration is never a good reason to quit. If I'm frustrated, I might walk away for a little bit, but I never throw in the towel just because I'm discouraged. If I think about what I'm doing and find it's not working because it isn't creating meaning, aligning with my values, or providing value for others, then I'll let it go.

Sometimes the work isn't worth the cost. I've fired clients because it wasn't a good fit for either of us. Our values didn't ultimately line up or we just couldn't communicate effectively. While it's never easy, sometimes cutting ties is necessary to free the other person to find someone else (so they get a better end result) and make room for projects that work better for you.

# Renewable resources

Our time and focus are not renewable resources. Once we use them, we don't get them back. This is why I say "no" a lot. I turn down design projects and writing assignments without remorse, because I know my work suffers if I overcommit. If I say yes to something, and my time and focus could be better spent elsewhere, I only have myself to blame.

Sometimes we can't say no – especially if we're starting out, because "no" might be something we have to work toward. "No" requires options – and mortgages, kids, commitments and other life situations can limit those options. But as we work at our craft and provide deeper value for our audience, more options often appear.

As you start to develop your craft and expertise, you tend to have much more time and focus. So, it's good to say "yes" to whatever work comes your way. As you get further along your path, though, your time and focus become more precious. You make the call about what to work on and what to skip, as this will ultimately shape how much meaning you find in what you do. Saying yes to the wrong things for too long will lead to work that lacks personal meaning.

There's a lot of responsibility in the option to say yes or no. It can be scary to say no, because it releases you from an opportunity. Turning down work is also turning down a paycheque. We fear there might not be other projects on the horizon if we say no to something right in front of us.

I say no so I can say yes to work that aligns with my values and what I love to do. I say yes to work that I'd happily sign my name on. I play the long game with yes and no, because creating a body of work takes a lifetime.

## Expertise & obscurity

You might feel like a fraud – like you aren't good enough to be doing the work you're doing, or like your opinion isn't valid because you're not an expert.

There aren't really any experts, though, just people further along in their individual journeys. I guarantee that they all feel like frauds sometimes, too. But if you're good at your work and people value your opinion, then congratulations—you're in the same group as the experts.

You don't need a degree, publishing deal or keynote speaking gig for validation. Confidence means simply believing in your work and hard-earned experience while acknowledging that you're never done learning. Experts can be wrong all the time. They can also be fearful.

You don't have to be right to be confident (politicians are a great example of this truth in action); you just have to understand something enough to have an opinion – and then you have to accept that it could be wrong and feel willing to change at any time.

If you don't yet have an audience that values your opinion, you're actually in a wonderful place. Revel in the obscurity, because it means you're free to try and fail without much attention. This is a great time to experiment with prototypes, try lots of wild ideas, and do potentially outlandish work. The experts have people to impress, many eyes watching their every move, and lots on the line.

Either place has its pros and cons, and people in each group sometimes wish they were in the other. The grass is always greener.

## Gatekeepers

In almost every industry, gatekeepers are disappearing. Gone are record deals, publishers and the investors that were previously necessary in order to share what we make. Now, we can connect directly with people in every corner of the world.

Let's take that new reality one step further: what if the world existed without publishers, record labels, investors, critics, and even internet trolls? What if it was illegal to judge anyone else's work? What would you make? This world can exist if you want to it be real.

We are free to share what we want, and all that's holding us back is ourselves. So what will you share?

## Be a maker

Without gatekeepers, we've all got simple public platforms to share our work, which has forced us to become promoters. This cuts into actual creation time and can sometimes overtake creation.

Social media promotion has become as ubiquitous as "Keep Calm and Carry On" memes. We're all so bombarded with promotion that we filter it out, rendering it useless.

For the first decade of working for myself, I didn't do any promotion. I didn't even use social media (as it existed back then in places like GeoCities). I focused on making the best possible websites for my clients.

Unfortunately, passion-focused business owners can be so passionate about what they do that they want to constantly tell everyone about it.

Doing well at something comes from iteration and innovation, not constantly promoting what you've already made. There's a place for spreading the good word, but it shouldn't take priority over generating ideas and creating killer new things.

## Theft & iteration

There weren't very many websites when I started doing design, but I used to look at their graphics and source code to see if I could replicate them. I would do this again and again until I could replicate the sites effectively. Then I would try to make them better, faster, and more in line with my own style.

I'd do this hundreds of times – all in the privacy of my own computer. Once I felt like I could effectively copy and replicate individual sites, I'd blend the best of several into one single site. I would replicate it again and again until I could do it quickly. Then I would try to fix the inconsistencies, since the design was pulled from multiple sources. I'd smooth those out so it'd look like a cohesive brand. Then I would work at making it look better and work more efficiently. I'd iterate on this process over and over again.

The end result wouldn't look anything like the sources I had originally copied, and this is how I taught myself to design and program – through theft and iteration.

Not much has changed since then. I still steal all my initial ideas from other sources. Sometimes it's the web, but mostly it's from nature, fashion, magazines, books, architecture, or art. If I see something that works for a project, I steal it. Small things. I iterate on details until they feel consistent. I iterate on specific elements until they fit my unique style. After these pieces survive my process, they don't resemble what I took in the first place – and if you compared the end result with the original source, you'd say, "really?"

## The difference between mimicking & theft

Most artists wouldn't consider my process "theft." Not every painting of a semi-smiling woman is a daVinci rip-off, nor is every website a copy of the first-ever site. If you're doing a similar thing, using the same medium, there will always be similarities.

Mimicking is taking something and passing it off as your own. This is bad – but not for the obvious reasons. It's bad because if you mimic what someone else does, you've failed to tell your story. Your story is the unique lens you use to create. It's what makes your work, your work.

Artists use other materials as a starting point to tell their own story. Everyone is influenced by someone who came before them. Creation doesn't exist in a vacuum.

When we're inspired, we don't have to worry about finding a muse in order to begin. Our muse lives in the work of others and it's literally everywhere. Use it as a base to build and refine your own, unique story and flavour.

It can be terrifying to stare at a blank screen and tell yourself, "Now create something great."

In the beginning, especially, I didn't concern myself with stealing. I was copying and emulating for educational purposes. I shamelessly stole to teach myself complicated things.

When I break it down, that's exactly how I've learned everything I know – not through school, but through theft and iteration.

## The process is ugly

Creativity is part magic. The bigger parts, though, require us to show up and iterate until there's a beautiful finished product.

The process required to move from first draft to final product is usually quite ugly. It takes many horrible drafts, bad ideas or paths that lead nowhere to arrive at something good. Just like the puzzle box, creativity doesn't work until it does.

We idolize creativity because, as consumers of it, we see only the finished product – the best version of something that may have taken days, weeks, months, or years to complete. That final product involved a lot of curation, editing and iteration until it was truly great.

All creative work includes a process that other people may never see. Good design or a polished product makes the process seem easy, when in reality it takes a lot of hard work. Writing a book is the same. If the end result is an easy read that flows brilliantly, chances are it took double-digit revisions, many edits and lots of tweaking to get it right. This can take months or even years to complete.

Good finished products aren't like social media updates – important for a second or two. They can last and be relevant for a lifetime (or longer).

Once you make your work public, it should feel rational—like it all adds up. My web and writing projects make sense only when they're done. They can be crazy, dirty, and messy until they're finished.

Brilliance and genius are usually iterative. Things don't work until they do. You don't need to be an expert at first; you can learn as you go.

The creative process is difficult and full of frustration. But "this isn't working" becomes annoying only if you're focused purely on the end goal. When something's done, it's for other people, but when you're working on it, it's just for you.

The process is where the magic happens. Enjoy the beauty of creating, inventing, exploring. Don't wait until it's finished to feel rewarded, since that might never happen. The labour *is* the reward.

## Create bad first drafts

Slogging through a first draft or prototype is tough for most creatives. Whether it's writing, designing, filming or anything else, it's always the same scenario. The first try isn't bad because the ideas aren't there; it's bad because it tends to be a mish-mash of every single idea and brainstorm we've applied to the project. There can be too many ideas, thoughts that don't make sense, and execution more suited to a toddler... that sort of thing.

In this stage, just get the ideas down and put your editing hat away. Brainstorm until there isn't anything left to brainstorm.

Create as badly as necessary to get things created. Editing, polishing and curating can all happen later.

I tend to almost purposefully write bad first drafts. They're hideous and something I wouldn't even show my editor. But I get the ideas down on (virtual) paper and move forward – and then I have something concrete to mold and shape.

By focusing on the idea instead of how the idea is presented, I can iterate later until it's ready for public consumption.

## Comparison is ugly

We've covered why the process is ugly. But it's also futile to compare our work with other people's creations, since we don't know or see their full process.

The end result can look easy, like it couldn't be any other way. But it took real effort to get there. You might never see what happened behind the scenes. There could have been sleepless nights or 108 auspicious iterations before coming to the "obvious" conclusion.

Comparison is difficult because we're trying to match our whole, flawed selves against a perceived "perfect" other person. It's comparing our personal reality to a fantasy version of someone else – and you can't match up two non-like things. Even if the situations were identical, *what purpose would the comparison serve?*

Enjoy the journey and the ugly process. It's yours. Stop measuring yourself against anyone or anything else and start examining what great work means to you.

## The end?

This isn't truly the end, because creating meaningful work isn't something that's ever done. It's constant—sometimes a struggle and sometimes it comes with ease. But it's never finished. No great artist has ever said, "well that last piece was pretty fucking epic, I'm going to call it right here." Even Jay-Z came out of retirement (several times, so far).

Making your own path is one of the scariest things you can do, because it makes you ultimately responsible for the outcome. You can't do it and then blame someone else if it doesn't work out. Fail or succeed, it's completely on you.

This book is truly everything I know (or at least, everything I know what's worth sharing). It's all here, and I hope you gain some insight from it. And clearly, it doesn't take long to read everything I know.

Trying to fit in is the safest thing we can do. But there's already too much fitting in. Choosing a unique adventure can sound hard and scary. So why should we bother? We could stay safe and do things the "normal" way. The tried and tested way. The way others have gone before us and found success.

Making your own path means walking into the dark without a flashlight (or flashlight app), but there's no other way to live a meaningful life guided by what you value – and everyone has different values.

Your work is not just about you; it's about the people who consume it. Finding where your own values and meaning align with what your audience is willing to pay for (your intersection) is magical stuff and can take a lifetime to achieve.

You might be scared on your path, sure. But the only way forward is to take a small step. Then another. And then another. Keep moving until it resembles walking or running. What you create is a reflection of yourself, so it gains meaning as it gets closer to your own magnetic north. Your internal compass points to what you value, so fail or succeed, stay true to that and you'll never get lost.

This isn't the end; this is the beginning. Forge a new path by taking a single step in a new direction. Staying true to your values requires you to constantly check in and re-evaluate what you're doing. Fears don't ever go away, but you can manage them and push on to do great work alongside your fear.

*You are responsible for the work you put into the world, so why not make that work great?*

# Epilogue

I realize that I tend to write a lot about negative emotions and experiences, like criticism. Fear. Failure.

Horribly un-uplifting (down-lifting isn't a word for a reason). My words are typically framed in the guise of overcoming and championing, which is my pessimistic way of getting to write what I want with only a glimmer of hope at the end.

So what happens in the absence of negative emotions? I'm not talking about finally overcoming all of those self-confidence trials and tribulations to become an egomaniac (that's another book altogether). But what happens when you find your "groove?" When you're sitting at your desk working and the muse actually shows up to whisper in your ear?

Inspiration. Genius. Revelation. Whatever you call it, the world (for all its faults), sometimes reveals works of beautiful art and moments of brilliance. Even thinking about the times when you've experienced that magic, in whatever large or small way, can give you goose bumps.

There's a constant struggle inside all of us to create something inspired and awesome.

The negative moments can make it feel impossible to achieve the open space and attention required for brilliant creation. We tell ourselves we can't or we're not good enough and then let all those criticisms, fears and failures stream in. They can consume us. But then sometimes they don't. Their defenses are not without cracks, and sometimes we see a light shining through and run screaming toward it with all our might, like a streaker across a football field.

How do we find our own genius? Why does it happen sometimes and not in other moments? Can the secret be bottled and sold as a travelling sideshow tonic? If so, sign me up for **ALL THE BOTTLES**.

I may not know how to create amazing work with every try (no one does), but I sure as hell know what it feels like, if briefly. There are pieces of writing, music and design I've done that I don't hate. Fleeting, proud moments. Those moments of inspiration make me feel like I'm myself (which shouldn't seem as foreign as it does). It feels like I've grasped my true voice and held onto it with all my strength, if only for a second. It feels a little frantic, too, as if the muse is always trying to get away.

But in those inspiring moments, I feel utterly present – so present that if I took even a microsecond to think about the feeling, I'd lose it. It's the sort of presence that holds no room for subconscious worries or multi-tasking thoughts.

In genius there is only space to do whatever the genius is channeling. A phone call, calendar notification or a stray thought about your Twitter feed grinds everything to a halt. Since the revelation is fleeting, like it has other places to be, the second you weaken your grip or lose the strength to hold on, it moves on – until someone else grabs hold tightly. Lucky bastard.

Here's the most interesting part: the *second* before it hits, right as the muse draws in her breath to whisper in your ear, is when all those negative thoughts and ideas reach their pinnacle. It's the absolute worst second of your life and you're at your most fearful. You might feel okay about writing until you sit at a keyboard and stare at a blank screen. You might feel like you can write a great song until you pick up that guitar and think about the first chord. Then you panic. Breathe more rapidly. You probably grab your phone and refresh Facebook instead of pushing through the fear.

This is the make or break moment – and the rub is, even if you start and become a conduit for inspiration in that second, nothing is guaranteed. You can start working and the genius might not arrive. But it's a numbers game, and your odds of doing great work increase only when you do more work. Keep at it and you may do great, inspired work. But if, in that moment, you go the easy path, the path of least resistance, the path that leads back to the same, tired place, then you missed your chance. You're back to staring at online cat or celebrity photos, and the possibility of doing great work returns to zero. It goes back to being a pipe dream, something for future attempts... for tomorrow.

Repeatedly summoning the courage or resolution to work can wear down your resistance. If you do something every day, routinely, your fears can diminish – not totally, not even majorly, but enough to notice. Those fears get tired of being ignored. They grow weary and maybe even bored. That's why it's typically easier to write the middle of the book than the first page, or to finish that last part of a painting than the initial brush stroke. Or to play the 32nd show versus the very first tour date.

**Attention is a gift you give to your work.** The more attention you devote to something, the less space fear can occupy.

Attention isn't just about avoiding your neuroses (always a good thing); it means you're absolutely present and ready for your genius. It means you can get down to work and if the muse is feeling talkative, the work might turn out brilliantly.

Genius might be trying to reach you *right fucking now*. Are you listening, or are you busy refreshing Twitter?

## About the author

Paul Jarvis is a web designer, best selling author and gentleman of adventure.

He's founded several start-ups, toured the US and Canada in the band Mojave, self-published two books, and has worked as a web designer for almost two decades.

Paul's writing appears in *Fast Company, The Huffington Post, Adobe's 99u, The Next Web, GOOD, Elephant Journal, Design Taxi,* Medium.com and many other publications. With an international reputation as the designer whose vision and web design strategy builds multi-million dollar businesses, he's worked with Fortune 500 companies, best-selling authors and the world's biggest entrepreneurs. Paul's clients include Yahoo, Mercedes-Benz, Microsoft, The Highline in New York City, Danielle LaPorte, Marie Forleo and Kris Carr.

You can find him on Twitter at @pjrvs. He currently lives in the woods on Vancouver Island with his wife Lisa and their two rats, Onha' and Awe:ri.

*He also thinks writing about himself in the third-person is kind of weird... but not in the "good weird" way.*

## Thanks

My wife, Lisa, for continuing to put up with an introverted, stoic and neurotic husband. Cheri Hanson for being brilliant with words and helping me put them together. Marc Johns for being able to make beautiful art. Justine Musk for the killer, inspiring foreword. Everyone else who has helped to make this possible with guidance, assistance, criticism and kicks in the ass.

*And you, the reader.*

To continue what we've got going here, hop on my mailing at http://pjrvs.com/signup or tweet at me @pjrvs.

You can also check out my other books—

*Eat Awesome* - www.eatawesome.ca

*Be Awesome at Online Business* - www.pjrvs.com/book

*Write & Sell Your Damn Book* - www.mydamnbook.com

Made in the USA
San Bernardino, CA
20 September 2014